Y0-DKP-907

Looking at GREAT BRITAIN

A farm surrounded by young hopfields. The buildings with
conical roofs are oast-houses where the hops are dried

Looking at
GREAT BRITAIN

LORNA HINDS

Adam and Charles Black   London

J. B. Lippincott Company   Philadelphia and New York

Lincoln Cathedral

Looking at Other Countries   *Titles in this series*

Looking at HOLLAND   **Looking at SPAIN**
Looking at ITALY   **Looking at FRANCE**
Looking at GREECE   **Looking at ISRAEL**
Looking at NORWAY   **Looking at SWEDEN**
Looking at DENMARK   **Looking at GERMANY**
Looking at JAPAN   **Looking at GREAT BRITAIN**

Further titles in preparation

Grateful acknowledgement is made to the following for their permission to reproduce photographs:

Margaret Baker 10, 11 b, 25, 36 b, 41, 42 b, 51, 58
Barnaby's Picture Library cover b
British Aircraft Corporation 61
British Steel Corporation 33
British Tourist Authority 7, 12 a, 12 b, 13, 15, 20 a, 21 a, 21 b, 22, 24, 27 a, 32 a, 32 b, 52 a, 52 b, 53, 57
Vincent Brown 43
Jarrold Colour Publications 2, 6, 11 a, 14, 18, 19, 23, 26, 27 b, 31, 35, 46, 47
Noeline Kelly 8 a, 8 b, 9, 17 a, 34 a, 34 b, 36 a, 37, 40, 45 a, 45 b, 60
Popperfoto 30, 50
Rover Company Ltd 28
Jonathan Rutland cover a, 1, 16, 17 b, 20 b, 36 c, 38, 39, 48, 54 a, 54 b, 59
E. Alistair Smith 42 a, 44 a, 44 b, 55, 56
The Times 49
Josiah Wedgwood and Sons Ltd 29

The cover pictures show an inlet on the northwest coast of Scotland and the fountains and National Gallery in Trafalgar Square, London

The maps on pages 62 and 63 were drawn by Specialized Drawings Services Ltd

U.S. Library of Congress Cataloging in Publication Data

Hinds, Lorna.
    Looking at Great Britain.

    (Looking at other countries)
    SUMMARY: An introduction to Great Britain—its people, history, customs, and industries—through a visit in text and photographs to various sites and cities.
    1. Great Britain—Juvenile literature. [1. Great Britain] I. Title.
DA27.5.H56 1973   914.2'03'85   73-5947
ISBN-0-397-31335-7

ISBN 0 7136 1339 4 (British edition)

© 1973 A & C BLACK LTD, 4, 5 & 6 SOHO SQUARE, LONDON W1V 6AD
PRINTED IN GREAT BRITAIN BY JARROLD & SONS LTD, NORWICH

CONTENTS

Decimal coinage was introduced in Britain in 1971. £1 (one pound) = 100 pence. A new design of 50-pence coin was minted in 1973 to mark Britain's entry into the European Common Market

Britain and the British

Great Britain is a very green island. Three-quarters of its area is farmland and there is plenty of rain to keep it green. Everywhere there are fields, leafy hedges and trees.

This is a man-made landscape, a patchwork of fields, each one enclosed by a hedge or a dry wall of local stone. Only the sandy heathlands, marshes, moors and mountain sides have been left relatively untouched.

The scenery is very varied. Most of southern England is gently rolling countryside, though the West Country is fairly hilly and has stretches of wild moorland. The Midlands are generally considered an industrial area, but here too are farms and orchards. To the east, particularly along the coast, East Anglia almost rivals the Netherlands for flatness.

The northern part of England is much more rugged, with mountains, upland pastures, lakes and moorland. Much of England's industry is concentrated here in towns and cities on rivers such as the Tyne, Tees, Humber and Mersey.

Kilnsey Crag, a famous landmark in the Yorkshire Dales National Park, an area of high moorland in the North of England

In Britain's highly industrialized society folk dancing and traditional customs are rare but some are kept alive by enthusiasts like these Morris dancers

The scenery of Scotland and Wales is rugged and mountainous too. The people of both countries speak English with very distinctive accents and in some remote areas people still speak Gaelic and Welsh. These are Celtic languages which have developed from those that were spoken in Britain two thousand years ago.

England, Scotland and Wales—three distinct countries— are all part of the United Kingdom of Great Britain and Northern Ireland. The three peoples, the English, the Scots and the Welsh, seldom think of themselves as British (and never as Britishers) and the Scots and Welsh object strongly to being called English.

The British have a reputation for being reserved. Strangers in the same railway compartment are quite likely to pass a long journey without saying a word to each other. The British have another reputation—for always talking about the weather. This is not surprising for Britain has nothing reliable enough to call a climate. It has weather.

Office workers waiting for a train in a London suburb   People waiting for a bus

Britain's weather is described as temperate. In practice this means that the British never know what their weather is going to be like for two days running. Winter weather can be cloudy, damp and warm, sunny with frost and snow, or frosty and foggy. Summer weather can be chilly and damp, or hot and sticky or, on a few glorious days each year, brilliantly sunny and warm with a flawless blue sky.

Perhaps the changeable weather has played its part in shaping the British character. People tend to accept what comes and to muddle through without getting excited. Pushing to get on a bus first or jumping one's turn to be served in a shop is frowned on. And "please", "thank you", "sorry" and "excuse me" are phrases children learn at an early age.

Of course, the British do get upset and argumentative sometimes, but there is rarely a serious clash. Both sides give way a little and a compromise is reached. Britain must be one of the very few countries to have avoided a bloody revolution or a civil war for over three hundred years, and the British find it difficult to understand the passions of their Irish neighbours, for instance, over politics and religion.

Life is comfortable for most people in Britain. Half the families in Britain have a car and almost as many own their own homes. And there is usually money to spare for holidays at home or abroad, for home improvements such as central heating, for entertainment and hobbies. A family does not have to worry about paying school fees as education in state schools is free. Medical care is free too, except for some limited charges, and there is help for families with little money coming in, for people who cannot work because they are sick or cannot find a job, and pensions for old people.

This system of social security, which is designed to protect people from hardship and distress, is not really free, of course. It is paid for by taxes of one kind and another which are paid by nearly everyone of working age. And it doesn't cover everything. Various societies are constantly at work, trying to persuade governments to revise the rules so that people who have been overlooked can be helped.

Countrymen at a cattle auction in the North of England

The Monarchy

Britain is a constitutional monarchy. This means that, although the sovereign, Queen Elizabeth II, is head of state, her power is restricted by tradition and the laws of Parliament. There is no written constitution, so in theory there is nothing to stop the monarch from taking over the government of the country, but in practice Queen Elizabeth has no real power.

The sovereign is also the head of the Church of England which, partly for religious, partly for political reasons, broke away from the Church of Rome in the sixteenth century.

The monarchy is a well-loved tradition in Britain and it ensures that the country has a head of state who is not linked to any political party or policy. People love the ceremonial that is associated with royalty, and there is also a real affection for the Queen and her family.

Queen Elizabeth has a very full diary of public engagements, of state ceremonies such as the Opening of Parliament or the Trooping of the Colour, of good-will journeys abroad and of official receptions for foreign statesmen and heads of state. If a town has a new bridge or shopping precinct, the Queen or some other member of the Royal Family may be asked to perform the opening ceremony. A royal visit means new paint everywhere and possibly a day's holiday for the school children.

Queen Elizabeth II with members of her family at an engagement in Scotland

The view from Westminster Abbey, looking across the Houses of Parliament to the Thames and the City of London

Troopers of the Royal Horse Guards on guard in Whitehall

London

London is enormous, a sprawl of homes, offices and factories which stretches 35 miles (56 km) from east to west and 27 miles (43 km) from north to south. More than seven million people live in London, mainly in the suburbs which were once towns and villages in their own right; but a good many still live in central London.

Four and a half million people work in London. Most large organizations and government departments have an office in London, even if their head-quarters are elsewhere. It is a place for students too, for London has three universities, teaching hospitals for doctors and nurses, the Inns of Court for law students, and schools of art, music and drama.

The first mention of London in history is by the historian Tacitus who noted that the Roman trading settlement of Londinium was destroyed in A.D. 61 by Boadicea and her tribesmen. It was a natural choice as a trading post as there was a ford across the Thames and good sea routes to Europe. During the Roman occupation (A.D. 43–410) London became Britain's most important town. Main roads radiated from it—they still do—to all parts of the country.

The area within the boundaries of the old Roman and medieval cities is now called the City of London. For a thousand years the City has been an important force in English history, respected by kings and nobles for its wealth and power.

The City is a tightly packed square mile of mainly modern office buildings. It is only when you look at the street names in and around the City that you get a glimpse of an earlier town where people lived as well as worked—Milk Street, Seacoal Lane, Vineyard Walk, Bowling Green Lane, Cloth Fair.

King's Bench Walk in the Temple (one of the Inns of Court where the lawyers who plead in the higher courts have their offices)

The coach which carries the newly elected Lord Mayor of London to the Law Courts to take the oath of office

BELOW LEFT Part of London's old city wall surrounded by new buildings

At night and at weekends the City is deserted (fewer than five thousand people actually live there) but in the daytime its streets are packed with businessmen and office workers. The wealth and power of the City come from banking, insurance and the selling of stocks and shares as well as from trade in goods and cargoes from all over the world.

The City handles millions of pounds' worth of transactions every working day. Many of these deals are made by word of mouth alone, however large the sums of money involved. This is a tradition that dates from the time when the business of the City was carried out in coffee houses. Lloyd's of London, for instance, which handles insurance of all kinds throughout the world, still remembers its origin as Edward Lloyd's Coffee House by calling its uniformed staff "waiters". The Stock Exchange does the same.

The City is a fascinating place to wander in. Glance through an archway in a gloomy street and you catch a glimpse of a beautiful courtyard belonging to one of the old craft guilds of London. Or you may see a magnificent car packed tight with people dressed in fur-trimmed robes and knee breeches, with cascades of lace at throat and wrist: the Lord Mayor and his retinue on their way to an official engagement.

13

St Paul's Cathedral

When London was rebuilt after the Great Fire of 1666 the City authorities rejected the plans of Christopher Wren (1632–1723) for a new city of squares and wide streets; they retained the medieval street plan and so prepared the way for London's traffic jams which were serious even in the days of horse buses.

Wren did, however, design fifty-two City churches and London's cathedral, St Paul's. Its huge dome dominates the City skyline and the great Renaissance church provides a setting for national ceremonies such as the state funeral of Sir Winston Churchill in 1965.

The Great Fire did not reach the east of the City where William the Conqueror (1027–87) had built a castle to protect and control London. The Tower of London (the name comes from the White Tower, the great central Norman keep) is one of the most splendid fortresses in Britain. Many famous people, Queen Elizabeth I (1533–1603) and Sir Walter Raleigh (1552–1618) among them, were imprisoned there; for others, such as Queen Anne Boleyn (died 1536) it was also a place of execution. Now it is a popular place for tourists who come to brush up their history, to study the magnificent collection of armour and to admire the Crown Jewels in their security vault, deep in the ground.

Less than a mile upstream from the City is Westminster which has been the seat of government for nine hundred years. Here the medieval kings had their palace and to it they summoned, about seven hundred years ago, the first parliaments. Two groups of men met to advise the king, the Lords (the great landowners and bishops) and the Commons (country gentlemen from the counties of England and businessmen from the cities).

Parliament still consists of Lords and Commons, but the Lords have little power these days. The House of Commons governs the country. Its 630 members are elected by everyone (with a few exceptions) who has reached the age of eighteen. There are two main political parties, Conservative and Labour. The leader of the party which wins an election becomes Prime Minister and forms a Cabinet of ministers who are responsible for making government policy and for carrying it out through their ministries or departments.

The leader of the party which loses an election becomes Leader of the Opposition, an official paid post, for it is felt that the party out of power has a valuable part to play in criticizing the work of the government.

Judges in procession at the Houses of Parliament

Most of the buildings you see when you visit the Houses of Parliament are not as old as they seem. One, however, is very old. Westminster Hall dates from 1099, and its wonderful wooden hammer-beam roof, the largest ancient roof in the world to be built without supporting pillars, was added in 1395.

Across the road is Westminster Abbey. Most of the present church was built in the thirteenth century, but there were important churches on this site for many centuries before. Since 1066, when William the Conqueror was crowned there, the Abbey has been the traditional setting for the coronation of British kings and queens and for royal weddings too. There are countless things to see in the Abbey: the exquisite fan vaulting of the Henry VII Chapel, the tombs and monuments of famous men and women, the life-size effigies of kings and queens, and the Coronation Chair which contains the Stone of Scone on which Scottish kings were once crowned.

The Houses of Parliament

The first thing many tourists plan to see is the Changing of the Guard at Buckingham Palace, the Queen's London home, a long and elaborate ritual of marching and counter-marching by men of one of the Guards regiments in their traditional uniforms of red tunics and black bearskins. When the new sentries are finally posted, the crowds drift away along the Mall, London's processional way, or into the parks which make the western half of central London so attractive.

Feeding pigeons in Trafalgar Square

Westminster Abbey

The tourist has two landmarks in finding his way round London. One is Trafalgar Square, with its statue of Nelson on top of a tall column. The other is Piccadilly Circus, a good starting point for exploration into the West End of London. From the Circus Regent Street curves north to the main shopping area. Piccadilly runs westwards between St James's and Mayfair and on to Belgravia and Knightsbridge, all elegant districts where many of the great houses have been turned into luxurious offices. Shaftesbury Avenue takes the opposite direction and leads to London's theatres and the scruffy but fascinating streets of Soho with its foreign restaurants and shops—Indian, Chinese, Turkish and Japanese, as well as French and Italian.

17

Finchingfield—a picture-book English village: houses, church, village green and a stream

Southern England

Many of the people who work in London live in towns and villages in the surrounding countryside. But the main concern of these areas is farming and market gardening, and the region is like an enormous well-kept garden. Everywhere you find the pattern of field and hedgerow, broken here and there by clusters of trees.

The villages can be charming with their crooked streets, old inns, village greens, duck ponds and ancient churches. Most of the cottages no longer house farm workers and craftsmen because British farming is a modern, highly mechanized industry with only a small work force. The new inhabitants, often from the city, lovingly restore the cottages, repair the plaster decorations and renew the thatched roofs.

There are big country houses too, often set in their own parks. Some are treasure houses of paintings and furniture; others are simple manor houses. Many of these houses are open to the public at weekends, and on a fine Sunday afternoon the houses and gardens are crowded with visitors.

The white cliffs of Dover, the first sight of Britain for many visitors from Europe, are part of the North Downs, one of several ranges of chalk hills in southeastern England (*down* is an old word meaning hill). From Dover the North Downs curve across the country south of London to Farnham, while the South Downs stretch in whaleback-shaped curves from Beachy Head, the most startling cliffs in the southeast, to Winchester.

There is some industry, especially round Chatham and Rochester on the River Medway, with coal mines near Deal, but most of this area is farming country with hop farms and fields of sheep, and in spring there are miles and miles of blossoming fruit trees.

Canterbury, the chief town of this part of southeast England, is famous for its cathedral where Archbishop Thomas à Becket was murdered in 1170. He was made a saint and in the Middle Ages people came from all over England to visit his shrine.

Butchery Lane, Canterbury, and the great central tower of the Cathedral

Jane Austen's home at Chawton, near Winchester—a typical eighteenth-century middle-class house

Brighton Pavilion, an architectural folly built by the Prince Regent, later George IV (1762–1830)

The south coast is studded with seaside holiday towns. Brighton in particular attracts people who are seeking a day's sunshine by the sea and those who enjoy poking round antique shops and admiring the splendid domes of the Royal Pavilion.

Sixty miles (96 km) along the coast to the west is the great transatlantic port of Southampton. It was from here that the Pilgrim ship *Mayflower* made the first part of its journey to America in 1620. Nearby is Portsmouth with its naval dockyard where HMS *Victory*, Nelson's flagship at the Battle of Trafalgar (1806), lies in dry dock and is now a museum.

To the north is Winchester, another beautiful cathedral city. It was once the capital of the Anglo-Saxon kingdom of Wessex, and later joint capital, with London, of the whole of England; the cathedral is the burial place of the Saxon kings of England. A more recent tomb is that of the great woman novelist, Jane Austen (1775–1817) who lived

20

much of her life in the Winchester area.

Between Winchester and the coast lies the New Forest which is, in fact, very old and contains some of the oldest oak and beech trees in England. The forest has been protected for nearly a thousand years and it is the home of hundreds of wild ponies which, until recently, roamed freely over the roads of the forest.

Twenty miles or so west of Winchester, Salisbury is an early example of an English "new town", for the cathedral and the neat grid of streets around it were built in the thirteenth century.

North of Salisbury there is a great spread of chalk downs, Salisbury Plain. Many of the prehistoric immigrants to Britain made their home here and the whole area is rich in prehistoric remains. The most famous is Stonehenge. Nobody is quite sure what Stonehenge was—perhaps it was a temple or a great tribal meeting place —but it is certainly more than three thousand years old.

Stonehenge

Salisbury Cathedral. The spire, the tallest in England, is 404 feet (123 m) high

Oxford

The Thames

The Thames, England's longest river, rises in the Cotswolds, a range of limestone hills which runs parallel with the River Severn and its great estuary on the west coast of southern England.

The first big town on the Thames' journey eastwards to London and the sea is Oxford, the home of one of Europe's oldest universities, dating from 1249, a medieval city of spires and ornate buildings and one of Britain's fastest growing industrial towns.

From Oxford the Thames winds its way through Reading to Windsor where it is overlooked by the splendid royal castle—

22

the country home of English kings and queens since William the Conqueror founded it in the eleventh century.

A few miles downstream are the riverside meadows of Runnymede where, in 1215, King John was forced by his barons to sign Magna Carta, in which he promised not to flout the laws of the kingdom. John had no intention of keeping his word, but in succeeding centuries the Great Charter could be used to prove that kings were subject to law just as much as their subjects, and so it is rightly regarded as one of the first steps in the development of democratic rule. At Runnymede too is the memorial to the American president, John F. Kennedy.

In London the Thames is a working river but soon it will have more pleasure boats than barges and ocean-going ships, for some of the London docks have been transferred downstream to the mouth of the river, and a flood barrier is to be built to protect London from high tides, giving London a giant boating lake.

Windsor Castle

The fishing port of Brixham

The West Country

Every summer all the roads to the West Country are jammed with cars, for the long south-west peninsula is England's most popular holiday region, partly because the climate is generally warmer and sunnier than elsewhere. There is scarcely any major industry there, except in and around Bristol, the West Country's main city. Most of the people who live in the West Country are farmers or fishermen, or they earn their living from tourism. There are a few big holiday towns, but most of the holiday-makers are looking for a picturesque village or farm-house to stay in, or a little fishing port with gaily painted houses rising in terraces above the wharves and jetty.

The north coast of the peninsula is mostly wild and rocky, with magnificent waves rolling in from the Atlantic for the surfers; the south side is milder and more sheltered. It was from Plymouth, now an important naval station and dockyard, that *Mayflower* finally set sail for America in 1620. Much of the land is used for farming but there are stretches of heather-covered moorland, with streams and rocky outcrops, bleak but magnificent—Dartmoor and Exmoor which, like the New Forest, have their own breeds of wild pony who enjoy themselves helping picnickers to eat their sandwiches.

The fine cliff scenery of the Cornish north coast at Bedruthan Steps

Cornwall, the southwestern part of the peninsula, is part of Celtic Britain and has close ties with Wales and Brittany (it was once known as West Wales), although the Cornish language only survives in the place names which are quite different from those of the rest of England.

Cornwall has its moor too, Bodmin Moor, with other stretches of bare upland as well. Round Bodmin and St Austell wide stretches of land have been turned into a moonscape by the piles of waste from the china clay quarries. Ruined chimneys and engine houses mark the places where tin mines used to operate, but these signs of industrial activity merge into the distinctive Cornish landscape and do not spoil it.

St John's College, Cambridge, from the Backs

East Anglia

East Anglia occupies the corner of southern England which bulges out into the North Sea between the Thames estuary and the Wash. This quiet farming region is one of the dryest parts of England, but the cold winds which sweep in from the Continent in winter make it also one of the coldest. The land is largely flat and in the Fens, near the Wash, much of the land has been reclaimed from the sea. Here the great tower of Ely Cathedral can be seen for miles. Round Spalding the bulb fields make a brilliant splash of yellow, red and pink every spring and attract visitors by the coachful.

Cambridge, just south of the Fens, is an old university town (the oldest college, Peterhouse, was founded in 1284), busy during term time with students hurrying to lectures on bicycles, and during the summer with tourists who come to admire the college buildings and to walk along the banks of the River Cam where the gardens at the back of the colleges, "the Backs", run down to the river.

Kersey—once famous for its kerseymere cloth, made from East Anglian wool

Norwich, to the northeast, is a delightful city, with many old buildings carefully preserved, a magnificent cathedral with a superb Norman nave and a castle which has been made into a museum.

There are a number of holiday resorts round the coast but in general the marshes, mud flats, sand dunes and shingle are left to the wild birds and the ornithologists who study them. The sea is constantly nibbling at some stretches of the coast and in places whole towns have disappeared.

There is good sailing on the river estuaries and on the Norfolk Broads, a series of shallow lakes linked by dykes and rivers.

Horsey Mill on the Norfolk Broads

27

Assembling Rover cars at a
Birmingham factory

The Midlands

The Midlands stretch across central England from Wales in the west to the Wash in the east. The area is best known for its industrial towns which are grouped on the iron and coal fields which provide them with power and raw material.

From Birmingham to Wolverhampton there is a stretch of concentrated industry—often referred to as "the Black Country"—chiefly concerned with turning metal into all kinds of objects but with great emphasis on cars and their components. In Birmingham, Britain's largest manufacturing city and second in size of population only to London, there are nearly fifteen hundred distinct trades and crafts—jewellery manufacture is one—so it is hardly surprising that the view from the motorway which cuts across the suburbs is nothing but an apparently endless sprawl of factories and workshops.

Birmingham was heavily bombed during the Second World War and so a large area of the city has been redeveloped—particularly round the Bull Ring, the point at which main roads meet and the heart of the original market town in medieval times. But the city still has its nineteenth-century town hall and other impressive civic buildings which reflect the city's prestige and local pride.

Coventry, a car-manufacturing town to the southeast of Birmingham, is famous for its magnificent modern cathedral, built to replace one destroyed by bombing.

A second industrial area, "the Potteries", lies to the north of the Black Country. England's main pottery and porcelain manufacturing area is concentrated round Stoke-on-Trent; Wedgwood, Minton and Spode are some of the famous names associated with the Potteries. Coal mining and steel production are important in this region too, with many light industries linked to them.

A third manufacturing area to the northeast is also based on a coal field, Britain's richest and most productive, and one shared by the Mid-

Decorating a Wedgwood plate

lands and the North of England. Nottingham and Derby are the main towns in the Midland part of the coal field and they produce a wide range of engineering products and other goods too—Nottingham lace, for instance.

Further south, lying beneath countryside which is famous for its fox hunting, there is Britain's most productive iron ore field. A new town has been built at Corby on this field to provide homes for the people who work at the steel works there, carrying out the complete process of turning iron ore into steel sheets, plates and bars. Other important Midland towns are Leicester for knitwear and Northampton and towns nearby for boots and shoes.

In spite of all this important industry and the factory towns, the Midlands is mainly farming country with dairy and beef cattle, sheep, pigs and a variety of cereal and other crops, and the towns are country ones, serving farming people.

Little Moreton Hall

Apart from a patch of stone building in the East Midlands, the characteristic architectural style of old houses in the Midlands is timber framing. In the West Midlands this takes the form of "magpie" timbering in which black wood and white plaster are sharply contrasted, and fine examples can be found in and around Ludlow, Shrewsbury and Hereford. On the northern verge of the region, Chester, once an important Roman fortress, still has its medieval walls. But many of the buildings in the Rows are timber-framed: the Rows are a unique feature of Chester, shopping arcades raised above street level where one can wander happily away from the rain and the traffic.

A famous beauty spot in the west of the area, near the Welsh border, is Ross-on-Wye. The Wye flows from the Welsh border, past Hereford and down to Ross-on-Wye, winding between wooded hills and making its most spectacular bends at Symond's Yat, before making its way south into the great estuary of the Severn.

A few miles south of Birmingham and its factories the River Avon flows across peaceful farming country, through the historic towns of Warwick, with its medieval castle, Evesham and on to Tewkesbury where it joins the Severn.

The best known of the towns on the Avon is Stratford-upon-Avon, the birthplace of William Shakespeare (1564–1616). There are many lovely old half-timbered buildings in the town, including Harvard House with its ornately carved timbers (the home of the mother of John Harvard, founder of Harvard University in the United States) and the house where Shakespeare was born, in Henley Street. This has been restored and is now a museum of exhibits connected with Shakespeare's life and work. The garden is planted with trees, flowers and herbs mentioned in his plays.

Nearby a large building rises impressively from the banks of the river—the Royal Shakespeare Theatre. Every year thousands of visitors come here from all over the world to see Shakespeare's plays performed.

A mile away, in the village of Shottery, is what one guide-book describes as "probably the most admired and picturesque building in the world": Anne Hathaway's Cottage (Anne was Shakespeare's wife).

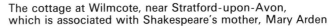

The cottage at Wilmcote, near Stratford-upon-Avon, which is associated with Shakespeare's mother, Mary Arden

31

A signpost in English and Welsh   Caernarvon Castle

Wales

The name Wales comes from Anglo-Saxon *Wealas* (foreigners).
The Welsh call their country *Cymru* (pronounced *Kuhmry*) which
means "land of comrades". Perhaps these names stem from the
fiercely independent character of the Welsh. In the Middle
Ages English kings had the greatest difficulty in subduing the
Welsh, and they were forced to build castles in strategic positions
all over the country in order to keep the Welsh under some sort
of control.

Even today, hundreds of years after the unification of
England and Wales, many Welshmen would like their land to
have its own parliament and its own language. In fact, many
people do speak Welsh and in a few parts, particularly in the
west, it is the first language. Newspapers and books are printed in
Welsh, and children learn English as a second language at
school.

Cardiff in the industrial south of the country is the capital
of Wales. It is a large seaport and one of Britain's main industrial
cities. It too has an ancient castle and it is the home of the National
Museum of Wales and the Welsh Folk Museum which recreates
Welsh life of the past in its exhibits of farm houses, rooms,
kitchens and dairies.

Well over half the people of Wales live in the industrial area of South Wales, most of them in Cardiff, Swansea and Newport, Wales' three largest towns. The development of South Wales as an industrial region began in the narrow valleys between the mountains with the mining of coal and iron ore. Wales' first iron works were at Merthyr Tydfil and Dowlais up in the valleys. Nowadays the steel works are on the coast and the ores for smelting and turning into steel are imported from all over the world.

Swansea has a giant oil refinery. Some of the crude oil arrives direct at Swansea's port but the giant supertankers can

Four miles (6 km) of steelworks at Port Talbot on the south coast of Wales

A coalmine in Ebbw Vale   Houses near Swansea

dock only in Milford Haven, sixty miles (96 km) to the west. From there the oil is piped to Swansea as well as to refineries at Milford Haven itself.

The coal-mining towns are tightly packed into the valleys, with the houses in terraces up the sides of the mountains. This is the home of Welsh singing, of male-voice choirs and of Welsh rugby football.

Some of the country's finest scenery is not far from the industrial belt—the Gower peninsula, with its towering limestone cliffs and sandy coves; and the Brecon Beacons, rising to nearly 3000 feet (900 m), to the north. Britain's largest castle, at Caerphilly, a few miles west of Newport, stands in the middle of a coalfield, and, a little further away to the east, the beautiful ruins of Tintern Abbey lie in a meadow on the banks of the River Wye.

Apart from the strip of lowland round the coast, the country is almost entirely mountainous. The highest peak is Snowdon, in the northwest, 3560 feet (1085 m) high; it is part of a mass of mountains shaped something like an octopus, with twelve lakes between the tentacles. Nearby are two other mountain masses, the whole region being known as Snowdonia. An area of craggy peaks, rocky passes, picturesque streams and lush wooded valleys, Snowdonia is one of Britain's most spectacular districts, and many people come here on holiday. For the experts Snowdon provides some really difficult climbs, but visitors can also walk to the summit or take the rack-and-pinion railway.

In central Wales engineers have created huge new lakes, some as reservoirs (Birmingham's water comes from here) and some as sources of hydro-electricity. But, apart from these modern projects, the countryside is lonely and windswept moorland where one can walk for hours without seeing another human being. There are a few sheep, and many ruined farmhouses; the farmers have either moved down to a valley where the land is more productive or have left to work in a town.

Although it is small, Wales has a thousand miles of coastline, with holiday towns and villages to suit all tastes. Llandudno and Rhyl are popular with holiday-makers from Manchester and Liverpool, while the west coast resorts are quieter. Aberystwyth, the chief town of West Wales, is the home of the University of Wales and of the National Library.

The southwest tip of the country has a windswept and rugged coast, yet because it is almost surrounded by the insulating Atlantic, it has the mildest climate in mainland Britain.

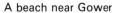
A beach near Gower

35

Old terrace housing built to cram as many workers as possible into the industrial towns

Semi-detached houses on the outskirts of London

Extra rooms in the roof

Homes

The English and the Welsh do not like living in flats or apartments. A young married couple make do with a flat in the first years of marriage—the upper floor of someone else's house perhaps—but they only do this until they can buy a house for themselves or rent one from the local town council. Tower blocks of flats are replacing acres of poor housing in London and other large cities, but people still hanker after a house with a garden where the children can play and the grown-ups snooze on a hot summer afternoon.

In Scotland town people have lived in flats for centuries and so more than half the housing there takes this form.

British houses are usually built in groups of identical design, linked together in pairs ("semi-detached") or long terraces to make the fullest use of the land available. Sixty per cent of British housing was built over thirty years ago, and the owners of these older houses

36

A summer afternoon in the back garden

are encouraged by grants of money from the government to bring them up to date. The British are very enterprising about improving their homes and the owners of even fairly new houses spend weekends and evenings installing central heating, double glazing, removing unwanted walls and chimneys and adding on extra rooms, as well as painting and decorating.

Styles of furnishing vary. Young people like modern furniture with clean lines, plain walls and carpets and plenty of space. Their parents probably feel happier with patterned carpets and wallpaper, more ornate furniture and all kinds of pictures and ornaments. Few people bother to have their furnishings all of one style and most homes are a comfortable mixture of old and new.

The average family house has a large living room, with possibly a dining corner, and a kitchen on the ground floor, and a bathroom and three bedrooms upstairs. There isn't much room to spare, and children may find it difficult to find a quiet warm spot to do their homework in.

Even in the centrally heated houses the living-room fireplace is the focus of family life and the television set, which provides most of the family's entertainment, is placed so that you can sit round the fire and watch television at the same time.

Education

The great thing about British primary schools is that children enjoy going to them. Tables are scattered about the classroom and at each three or four children will be working together on some project, idea or problem. The children will be talking to each other, discussing what they are working on, and the teacher will be moving around the room wherever she is needed, encouraging the children to ask their own questions and to find their own answers.

Children in Britain have to go to school from the age of five until they are sixteen. The primary stage lasts from five until about eleven, and after that children move on to a secondary school. Some areas have a large comprehensive school which takes all the children in the district. Most comprehensives have large modern buildings, with a wide range of modern equipment and have a thousand or more pupils.

Primary-school children in the playground of their school

Children working in small groups

In other areas the more academically minded children go to a grammar school where they will be expected to work hard, pass examinations, and probably try to get into a university. The less academic children go to a "modern" school where more time is spent on practical and vocational subjects.

The school day lasts, with breaks, from nine till four. Each school is free to choose what it teaches, the methods it uses and the examinations its students take. Most take an examination at fifteen or sixteen, and those who need higher qualifications for university entrance or particular careers take another at eighteen or nineteen. At first each pupil studies a wide range of subjects in both the arts and sciences but by the time he reaches the sixth form (the top class in a British secondary school) he may only be taking two or three.

Games and gymnastics are traditional subjects in the time-table, but dancing, judo, fencing, sailing and other activities can also be found in some schools; and teachers' enthusiasm for a particular activity—astronomy, electronics, local history, archaeology, for instance—may give rise to club and class activity for the students.

Secondary-school girls working in the school library

Some young people leave school as soon as they can, at sixteen, but many continue their education at school or at a college of further education for one, two or three years, to prepare for a career or for entrance to university, to a college of education (for future teachers) or some other form of specialized training for a career. Those who enter industry or certain trades or crafts often have the chance to spend one day a week at a technical college, learning the theoretical side of their jobs. Others take evening classes.

Increasing numbers of students are going to university. For many this means living away from home for the first time. Some go to one of the old-established universities such as Oxford, Cambridge or St Andrews, or younger ones like London, Durham or Leeds, while others study at one of the brand-new ones such as Sussex or Essex.

For those who cannot go to university when they leave school, there are external degree courses through home study and evening classes and there is the new Open University which works through correspondence lessons, television lectures and summer schools.

Food

The British like good plain food—"meat and two veg." is the ideal, and Sunday lunchtime sees this meal at its best— roast beef, lamb, pork or chicken, with baked potatoes and green vegetables, and perhaps a batter pudding baked in the meat fat and eaten with the meat.

Weekday meals tend to follow the same pattern. Sunday's meat may reappear in several forms, but there may be chops, sausages, stews, meat puddings and pies, fish or salads. Some eat their big meal at midday, others in the evening. A sweet course may follow, anything from home-made apple pie with cream to canned fruit and ice cream. In the North and in Scotland the evening meal is often called "high tea" and the main course is followed by the cakes and scones at which the local bakers and housewives excel.

The British breakfast is world famous, though few people have time to eat it on a weekday and make do with toast, corn-flakes or a boiled egg. But on holiday or at weekends the British relax and may work their way through three courses: grape-fruit, cornflakes or porridge (a Scottish speciality made from oats); bacon and egg, with perhaps sausages, mushrooms, tomatoes or fried bread; and finally toast and marmalade.

Cakes, buns and scones for tea-time eating

Sea-food stalls are popular at the seaside and in street markets

A quick snack from the fish and chip shop

People in the southern part of the country eat their cakes and pastries at afternoon tea, an old-fashioned meal which still survives in some families at weekends and on high days and holidays. There are plenty of cakes to choose from—sticky ones, fruity ones and many others. Holiday-makers in the West Country delight in cream teas: the local clotted cream spread on bread and eaten with jam.

The British drink a great deal of tea and coffee. A housewife may get through ten to twelve cups of tea during the day, from the first one as she gets up in the morning to the last one before she goes to bed. Coffee replaces tea in many families and is drunk almost as frequently.

The British seldom expect to find better food in a restaurant than they would eat at home, but they do trust their local fish and chip shop which sells deep-fried fish and potatoes to take home or to eat at once, straight out of the paper bag.

New buildings round Piccadilly Station, Manchester

The North of England

Many people think of the North of England as primarily a region of gloomy factories and rows and rows of meagre houses, hastily built for the people who crowded into the manufacturing towns in the late eighteenth and early nineteenth centuries.

The cotton trade was one of the first to be mechanized and to make use of powered machinery. Raw cotton arrived from America at the busy port of Liverpool on the Mersey river and was taken to mills in towns such as Preston, Bolton, Oldham, Blackburn and Stockport to be made into cloth. Then the finished fabric was exported all over the world from Manchester which became at that time the second town in Britain. The world's first passenger railway, opened in 1830, ran across the marshy plain between Manchester and Liverpool and, when the Manchester merchants thought they were being overcharged by the Liverpool dock owners, they built the Manchester Ship Canal, making Manchester into one of England's main ports.

Cotton is still important to Manchester but many other industries have been established, including engineering, man-made fibres and chemicals.

Unloading meat in Liverpool
docks

Pierhead, Liverpool

Liverpool has grown steadily and is now one of the world's busiest ports. In 1700 it was only a small town but a century later it had a population of over seventy thousand, and nearly five thousand ships sailed up the Mersey each year. Many of the ships were slavers, buying slaves in Africa and shipping them to the New World. When the slave trade stopped, cotton became Liverpool's big money maker.

People flooded into the city, hoping to make their fortune or to get a passage to America. Hundreds of thousands of Irish people arrived, escaping the potato famine of the 1840s, and Liverpool became hopelessly overcrowded and full of slums.

Most of the slums have now been cleared and there are many fine modern buildings and developments, but Liverpool is still a place where people are always arriving or leaving, a tough unsettled city but one full of life and energy.

Wool, not cotton, was the great industry east of the Pennines. The grassy uplands provided pasture for sheep and the rivers tumbling down the Pennine valleys provided power for the mills which turned wool into cloth. These days most of the wool is imported from the Commonwealth but the woollen industry, in towns such as Bradford, Leeds and Huddersfield, continues to produce cloths for export all over the world.

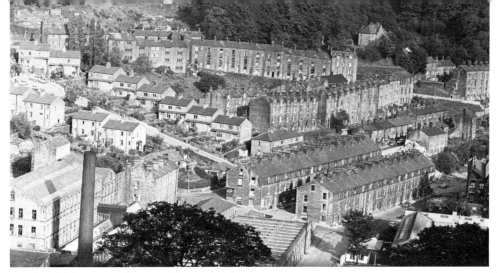

Hebden Bridge, a small town whose clothing
factories specialize in making men's trousers

Leeds also produces a good deal of Britain's ready-made
clothing, particularly men's suits and coats, and it is an engineering town too, as are Sheffield and Doncaster further south.
Sheffield, in particular, is famous for its high-quality steel and
its cutlery.

Half the fish caught by British trawlers is landed in the
Humber estuary on the east coast at Hull, one of the largest
fishing ports in the world, and at Grimsby. The Humber fishing
fleets sail as far as Newfoundland and Greenland for their
catches for sale as fresh fish and as frozen and, of course, as
fried fish with chips.

High Withens, near Haworth, the original of "Wuthering
Heights" in Emily Brontë's novel of that name

A major complex of heavy industry is based on the valleys of the Tyne and Tees rivers in towns such as Newcastle-upon-Tyne, with its engineering and shipbuilding, Middlesbrough, Stockton-on-Tees and Darlington. One of the largest chemical industries in Europe has been built up on Teesside.

Yet throughout the North the countryside is never far from the heart of the smokiest industrial town and young people go climbing, walking, camping, canoeing and caving, enjoying the wild and magnificent scenery of the Pennines, the Peak District, the Yorkshire Dales and the North York Moors, and making full use of the network of youth hostels provided in this as in other parts of Britain. Wide areas of the mountain and moorland have been made into national parks where the natural beauty of the landscape is carefully preserved. The really energetic can follow the Pennine Way, Britain's first long-distance footpath, 250 miles (400 km) long and stretching from the Peak District in the south to the Scottish border in the north.

Richmond, a small market town on the eastern side of the Pennines

Elterwater Tarn (lake) and Langdale Pikes in the Lake District

The Lake District, where the poets Coleridge (1772–1834) and Wordsworth (1770–1850) lived and worked, is on the west coast, south of the Solway Firth. The lakes are not particularly large and the mountains rise only a little above 3000 feet (900 m), yet the effect is spectacular and the scenery as varied and beautiful as any in Britain. Although it has one of the heaviest rainfalls in the country, it is a popular area for holidays, particularly for those who enjoy walking.

Holiday-makers on the promenade at Brighton

Holidays and Leisure

Most people in Britain have from two to four weeks' paid holiday each year and about 60 per cent of them go away for one or two weeks, usually to the sea (no place in Britain is more than 60 miles (96 km) from the sea). Sunshine is eagerly sought and so about six million go abroad each year, looking for it on the Mediterranean coasts. The rest crowd into Britain's holiday resorts which range from simple fishing villages and quiet seaside towns to big noisy places like Blackpool, Brighton, Llandudno and Ayr, full of bright lights and with plenty of things to do and see.

A small but increasing number of people now have the time and money to combine a holiday with sports such as sailing, riding or skiing. At home they can take part through classes or clubs and societies in a wide range of sports and other activities such as football, golf, tennis, squash, swimming, fishing, photography, amateur dramatics, music and gardening.

Professional sport is exceedingly popular. Television and newspapers devote a large part of their coverage to football, horse racing and boxing. In summer tennis dominates the sports news for the two weeks of the Wimbledon championships, and from late April to September cricket commentaries on television and radio convince people that it is summer, even though the weather outside may be wintry.

Cricket is a very English game and, like so many things English, it is very old. The rules have hardly changed since 1774. It is a leisurely and dignified game, played on village greens or on long-established cricket grounds which often have beautiful settings. Professional matches last for several days, though school and village ones are much shorter, and are broken up by lunch and tea intervals as well as by passing showers.

However, it is football, particularly association football, which obsesses small boys who kick a ball round the school playground and dream of playing for a famous club, and which keeps their fathers arguing for hours on the train or in the pub or canteen. Rugby has its fans but soccer mania affects the whole country.

Village cricket

Hadrian's Wall

The Border

For centuries the lands along the English-Scottish border have been the scene of battles and feuds. The Romans had so much trouble with the fierce tribes in Scotland that, during the first and second centuries A.D., they built a great wall and ditch, reinforced by forts, each of which was a small town, and other defence posts, to keep the invaders out. Hadrian's Wall (it was named after the emperor who completed it) stretched from the Solway Firth, a great estuary, in the west to the Tyne mouth in the east. A good deal of the wall survives and in stretches it is possible to walk along the path which runs along the top of it. For part of its course it runs along a great crag of rock and gives magnificent views of the bleak but beautiful countryside to the north and south.

Scotland

In 1603 James VI of Scotland became king of England (as James I) and in 1707 the two countries were joined by the Act of Union. Scotland lost its own parliament but it retained and still has its own national church and its own legal and educational systems.

The country is roughly divided into highlands and lowlands. The only real low land in Scotland is the broad strip which runs northeast from Ayr through Glasgow to Perth and Dundee and north along the coast to Aberdeen, but even in this region there are mountains and hills.

To the south there is an area of rolling uplands, with grass-covered hills, stone walls and isolated farms, very similar to the countryside south of the border in England.

To the north lie the Highlands, a Celtic area where Gaelic is still spoken, the home of the Scottish clans, groups of families who all bear the same name and owe allegiance to a chieftain. Highland dress—the kilt and sporran (the purse worn with the kilt)—is often seen in the streets of the little Highland towns and is worn by many men at country dances and parties.

Highland games at Braemar in the Cairngorms, a mixture of modern athletics and traditional Highland contests

A quiet close in the Old Town

A pipe band performing on the parade ground below Edinburgh Castle

Edinburgh, Scotland's capital, is a city of hills and splendid views and has a feeling of light and spaciousness which is surprising, considering that almost all the buildings are of sombre grey stone.

Dominating Edinburgh from its commanding position on top of a steep rocky ridge is the ancient castle. It is here on the parade ground, during the annual Edinburgh International Festival of Music and Drama, that the Scottish regiments, many wearing the kilt, perform their spectacular Tattoo, a military display with particular emphasis on the bagpipes and Scottish dancing.

On the slopes of the ridge lies the Old Town, an area of narrow lanes and picturesque old houses which seem very foreign to English eyes, for their stepped gables, little turrets, dormer windows and steeply pitched roofs are very different from the architecture south of the Border.

The lack of space in the old walled Edinburgh was responsible for its being the first

52

A panorama of Edinburgh with the Castle on the left, the monument to Sir Walter Scott on the right, and Princes Street on the far right

city in Europe to develop the system of living in flats or apartments. Even in the eighteenth century the houses were sometimes ten to twelve floors high.

The main street of the Old Town is known as "the Royal Mile". Running from the Castle to the Palace of Holyroodhouse, once the home of the Scottish kings, it passes the Cathedral Kirk of St Giles (the central church of the Church of Scotland) and the old Parliament House where the Scottish Parliament met until England and Scotland were united in 1707.

Princes Street, the city's main shopping street, marks the southern boundary of the New Town which was built in the eighteenth century, an area of elegant streets and squares and an early and beautiful example of town planning. One side of Princes Street is lined with large and imposing shops where visitors delight in buying Scottish tartans, fine tweed cloths and sweaters of Scottish wool, and even kilts. The other side of Princes Street is open to the gardens which occupy what was once the North Loch (lake) and divide the Old Town from the New.

Old and new blocks of apartments in Glasgow

Glasgow, 44 miles (70 km) to the west of Edinburgh, is Scotland's largest city and its greatest area of industry. It owes its prosperity to the River Clyde which, until recently, was lined by the world's greatest ship-building yards. Glasgow has fine streets and squares of houses built by prosperous merchants two hundred years ago in the middle of the town. All around old slum areas are being demolished and their place taken by tall modern blocks of apartments. These new developments, together with the building of factories and motorways, are changing Glasgow into a modern industrial city.

Loch Achray in the Trossachs

Just half an hour's drive from Glasgow the road leads round the banks of Loch Lomond, one of Scotland's loveliest lochs, and on to the Trossachs. The name means "the bristly country" which aptly describes this region of heather-covered heathland, mountains and lakes.

A popular holiday area in the Highlands is the Dee Valley. The Dee rises in the Cairngorms and flows eastwards to Aberdeen, famous for its fishing fleet and granite quarries, and now the base for the exploration and exploitation of the North Sea oil fields.

The Dee Valley is a beautiful area of mountains and heather-covered hills, the home of herds of deer who startle the night driver by darting across the road in front of him. The Dee and its tributaries are noted salmon rivers, and visitors spend hours watching the fish battle their way upstream against the fierce rush of the water.

This is sheep country with lambs and their mothers wandering everywhere in the late spring. The valley farms have cattle too, bred for beef rather than milk, and this is the pattern throughout the coastal areas of this part of Scotland, from Inverness round to the Firth of Forth.

A wintry walk in the Cairngorms

The Highlands are split into two by a huge rift valley, the Great Glen. At the northern end of the Glen is Inverness, the chief city of the Highlands, and in the valley itself is Loch Ness. Some people believe that a great sea monster lives in the depths of the loch. At the southern end of the valley, near Fort William, is Britain's highest mountain, Ben Nevis (4406 feet—1343 m).

For the most spectacular scenery one must travel up the west coast, round Loch Maree to Ullapool, and on to the north-west tip, Cape Wrath. The roads are narrow and make wide detours round the countless lochs which cut into the coastline like the fjords of Norway. Very few people live in this part of Scotland and, apart from fishing and some sheep farming, the main source of income is tourism.

Parallel to the Great Glen is the Spey Valley, one of Scotland's leading holiday areas, which is being developed to provide outdoor holidays of all kinds: skiing in the winter and pony trekking, walking, bird watching, fishing, climbing, sailing and canoeing in the summer.

Eileen Donan Castle in the northwest of Scotland

Festivals

In England and Wales the great festival of the year is Christmas. A week or so before 25 December children start making paper chains and other decorations; their mother orders a turkey and a Christmas tree; presents are bought and Christmas cards sent to friends and relations. In the country children go off to pick sprigs of holly, with its red berries, and mistletoe.

Then on Christmas Eve everyone helps to decorate the house and to set up the tree with its tinsel and candles. In the evening groups of children go

Handbell ringers and carol singers touring a village at Christmas

from house to house singing carols. In most families the children hang a stocking (or a pillow case) at the foot of their bed, and once they are asleep their parents fill the stocking with presents. Some families prefer to open big presents round the tree after lunch but others fill the house with noise and piles of discarded paper and string at six o'clock in the morning.

Christmas dinner, eaten at midday, is the main event of the day: roast turkey, stuffed with chestnuts, followed by Christmas pudding and mince pies (both these traditional Christmas dishes are rich and dark with dried fruit and spices). In the afternoon, as it gets dark, the candles on the tree are lit, and more presents are opened, and there is yet more food—Christmas cake (a rich fruit cake) and the usual afternoon cup of tea.

Collecting pennies for the guy before
Bonfire Night

In Scotland presents are given at Christmas but the main celebration comes on New Year's Eve: Hogmanay. At the stroke of midnight everyone sings *Auld Lang Syne* and the "first footer" comes in. It is thought to bring good luck if the *first* person to set *foot* in the house in the New Year is dark-haired, so a dark man is chosen and stationed outside the front door until the clock strikes twelve. Then he brings in the traditional gifts of bread and coal. The party will go on for the rest of the night, with a good deal of whisky drinking and wandering from house to house. Luckily New Year's Day is a holiday for the Scots and for a good many other people too, who take the day off, unofficially.

Children love Guy Fawkes Night, 5 November. In theory it commemorates the failure of a plot to blow up Parliament. In practice it gives children the excuse for making a guy or effigy out of old clothes, hawking it round the streets or the houses nearby and extorting money from grown-ups. This they spend on fireworks which are set off as the guy is burned on a giant bonfire.

In the North Mischievous Night is celebrated on 4 November and all sorts of tricks are played: knocking on doors and running away, hiding gates and dustbin lids.

History

The early history of Great Britain is of invasions—Celts, Romans, Angles, Saxons, Norsemen and finally, in 1066, the Normans. The history of the Middle Ages is of constant attempts by the kings of England to keep control of England, to subdue Wales and Scotland, and to fight off attempts by powerful noblemen to restrain the power of the king.

During these struggles two important things were happening. The people of England, from all their varied origins, were becoming a single nation, the English, with a new language descended from

Hampton Court Palace, on the Thames near London, was a royal home and the scene of many important political events

Anglo-Saxon, Norse and Norman French. And the English parliament was slowly developing and growing in influence and power. By the sixteenth century one of the first requirements of a successful monarch was to be able to keep Parliament on his side.

Elizabeth I (1533–1603) managed this well but her successors, the Stuarts, had high ideas about "the divine right of kings". Charles I (1600–49) and Parliament came into direct conflict in 1642. Parliament won the civil war that resulted, and a republican government was set up. This proved just as tyrannical as previous governments, so in 1660 the Stuarts were brought back.

The landscape created by the Industrial Revolution

Britain has had a monarch ever since, but during the last three centuries it has been gradually established that power lies not with the sovereign but with government ministers who are responsible to an elected Parliament.

Britain has always been a trading nation but in the sixteenth century the discovery of the New World's riches encouraged British ships to sail further afield to look for new cargoes and new markets. The merchants of London and other cities found that financing an expedition to the New World or to Africa for a cargo of slaves could bring in greater profits than merely buying and selling goods at home. Many of Britain's colonies were acquired haphazardly as a result of trading ventures of this kind.

In the second half of the eighteenth century Britain became the world's first industrial nation. Her population, increasing rapidly, needed food. Her factories needed raw materials and markets for their products. And so Britain sought new territories abroad which could satisfy these needs. This was the origin of the British Empire. It seemed perfectly natural to the British then that large areas in Africa and elsewhere should be ruled from London, and that in world affairs Britain should represent one quarter of the world's population.

But today Empire has changed to Commonwealth, a loose association of independent and equal nations which recognize the British monarch as their symbolic head and which share in varying degrees a common language and culture. And Britain, after playing a major part in two world wars in which she exhausted her resources and her economy, has seen other countries overtake her in industrial success. It has been difficult for the British to adjust to the idea that they are no longer as powerful as they used to be, and that it is the United States of America, the Soviet Union and China which are the great dominating powers of world politics.

Now Britain is changing direction and moving into closer union with the countries of Western Europe in the Common Market, a prospect that alarms some Britons and excites others.

Fitting British traditions, practices and ways of thinking into a European framework—even the English Channel which has kept Britain distinct from Europe for so long may be by-passed by a tunnel—will make great demands on the British qualities of adaptability, compromise and tolerance. But no doubt the British will come through this testing experience successfully, having adjusted their ancient institutions and long-held customs to the new conditions in the way they have been doing for centuries.

Concorde—the Anglo-French supersonic airliner which is to some extent a symbol of Britain's new links with Europe

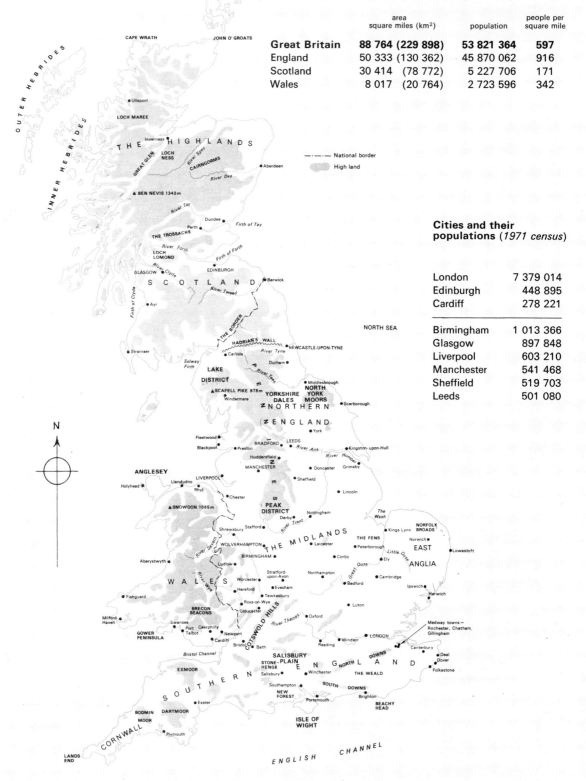

Some Facts and Figures (1971 census)

	area square miles (km²)	population	people per square mile
Great Britain	**88 764 (229 898)**	**53 821 364**	**597**
England	50 333 (130 362)	45 870 062	916
Scotland	30 414 (78 772)	5 227 706	171
Wales	8 017 (20 764)	2 723 596	342

- · - · - National border

High land

Cities and their populations (1971 census)

London	7 379 014
Edinburgh	448 895
Cardiff	278 221
Birmingham	1 013 366
Glasgow	897 848
Liverpool	603 210
Manchester	541 468
Sheffield	519 703
Leeds	501 080

N

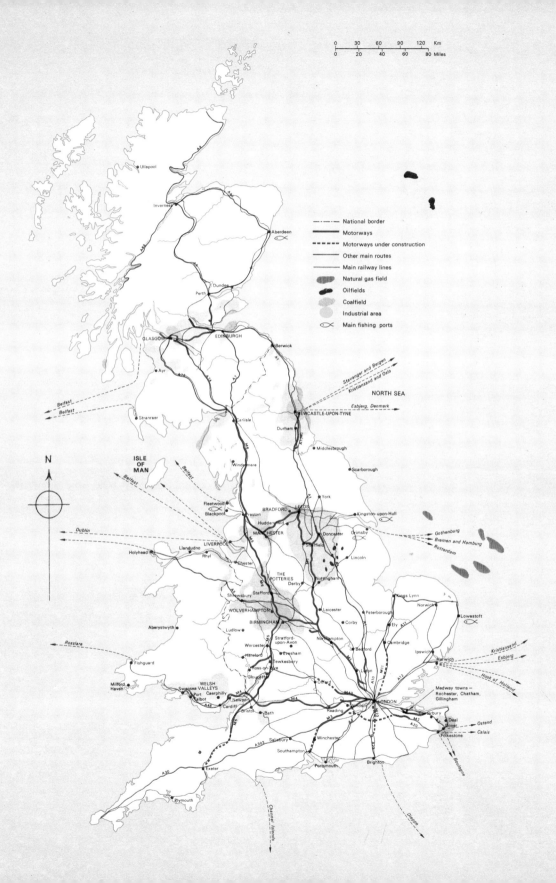

	Km
0 30 60 90 120	Km
0 20 40 60 80	Miles

National border
Motorways
Motorways under construction
Other main routes
Main railway lines
Natural gas field
Oilfields
Coalfield
Industrial area
Main fishing ports

Ullapool

Inverness

Aberdeen

Dundee

Perth

GLASGOW   EDINBURGH   Berwick

Ayr

Stranraer   Carlisle

Stavanger and Bergen
Kristiansand and Oslo

NORTH SEA

Esbjerg, Denmark

NEWCASTLE-UPON-TYNE

Durham

Belfast
Belfast

ISLE OF MAN

Belfast

Windermere

Middlesbrough

Scarborough

York

Fleetwood
Blackpool   Preston

BRADFORD   LEEDS
Huddersfield

Kingston-upon-Hull

Dublin

Llandudno
Rhyl

MANCHESTER

Gothenburg
Bremen and Hamburg
Rotterdam

Holyhead   Chester

LIVERPOOL

Sheffield   Doncaster   Grimsby

Lincoln

THE POTTERIES
Derby

Nottingham

Shrewsbury   Stafford

Kings Lynn
Norwich   Lowestoft

Aberystwyth

WOLVERHAMPTON
BIRMINGHAM

Leicester

Peterborough

Corby

Ely   A11

Ludlow

Stratford-upon-Avon

Northampton

Bedford   Cambridge

Rosslare

Worcester   Evesham
Hereford   Tewkesbury
Ross-on-Wye

Luton

Ipswich   Harwich

Kristiansand
Esbjerg

Fishguard

Gloucester

Oxford

M11
A10
A12

Hook of Holland

Milford Haven

WELSH VALLEYS
Swansea   Caerphilly
Port Talbot   Newport
Cardiff   Bristol   Bath

Reading   LONDON
Windsor

Medway towns –
Rochester, Chatham,
Gillingham

Canterbury
Deal
Dover

Ostend
Calais

Ostend

M2
A20

Salisbury
Winchester

Southampton

M3

Folkestone

A303

Portsmouth   Brighton

Boulogne

A30   Exeter

Plymouth

Channel Islands

Dieppe

Index

C 1

914.2   Hinds, Lorna
Hi
         Looking at Great
         Britain

DATE DUE			
FEB 25 '80			
Mill			
FEB 12 '85			
OCT 25 '85			
MAR 18 '86			
APR 23 '86			